# Pure Thoughts

by

Joseph Swain Jr.

DORRANCE
PUBLISHING CO
EST. 1920
PITTSBURGH, PENNSYLVANIA 15238

Dorrance Publishing Co
585 Alpha Drive
Suite 103
Pittsburgh, PA 15238
Visit our website at *www.dorrancebookstore.com*

ISBN: 978-1-4809-1287-8
eISBN: 978-1-4809-1609-8

This book is dedicated to

my wife, Tina,
whom I know God led me to her, I love you eternally;
my father, Joseph Swain Sr.;
my mother, Joann Swain;
my sisters, Phyllis and Sherice;
my strong sons, Joseph, Tyrelle, and Latrelle, Thomas,
and daughters Tricey and Marlene;
my best friend, Lloyd Wright, who is a very kindhearted and gifted person.

# Contents

# Pure Thoughts

# Inner Conflict

I see a black man approximately 180 pounds, 5'11", dark brown sad eyes.
He looked as if there is something heavy on his mind.
I tried to peer into his soul and what I saw scared me.
I saw a gifted, sensitive child who had been scared in his formative years
and never had the chance to let his real personality develop.
It looked as though this man was crying out for help
but didn't know how to ask for it.

Come here, child, I'll comfort you.
You can cry when you're blue.
No man is an island; no one stands alone
Communicate your fears till they're all gone.

# Gonna Follow My Dreams

I feel my dreams are so far away
That I might not ever reach them.
But with a longing desire, I must say
I'll have my dreams in me day by day.

My destination brings me closer to me
I got to keep on going with all my will.
My eyes are yearning to see
What my heart can only feel.

I'm gonna follow my dreams forever
I'm praying and hoping that they will lead me.
To bringing me and my fantasies together
To live forever together in harmony.

And if by chance I do succeed
You will surely see it in my eyes.
For my dreams they do lead
To keeping my spirit willing to try.

I have fallen so many times
Some people say I was born to lose.
But there's plenty of hope in my mind
To change those gray skies to blue.

## POSITIVE

New train of thought
Different way to walk
Imagination and reality
Greater possibilities

Not thinking of the bad
Not always feeling sad
To raise my self-esteem
Positive is my theme

Let the sun shine through
Dreams will come true
I am ready to live
Cause I'm thinking positive

# Reality

You know nothing worth having comes easily,
It's a basic fact called reality.
It took me a while to learn that fact,
But now I think I'm on the right track

I used to fantasize about being a big star,
While sleeping all the times, I wasn't getting far.
Now my eyes are open and I do believe,
You got to work hard if you want to succeed.

# Family

Family is joined together by blood
Family makes it together by love
And generation after generation
We share with old and new ones

Family may not always agree
But still love—that's the key
Day after day, year after year
We share the joy and the tears

When you need help, family is there
Guiding you with patience and care
So as for me, it is easy to see
I would be nowhere without my
Family

# Blue

A sophisticated illusion
Of mental confusion
Where did it all begin?
Was it my first sin?
Agony enough for two
Expressions to blue.

Day after day, year after year,
Inner conflict, silent tears.
Flesh and mind—which is right?
Difference between day and night.
What's the difference between one and two?
My conscience is making me blue.

Trying to live right
A tremendous fight
God, come to my aid
`Cause today I'm in a daze.

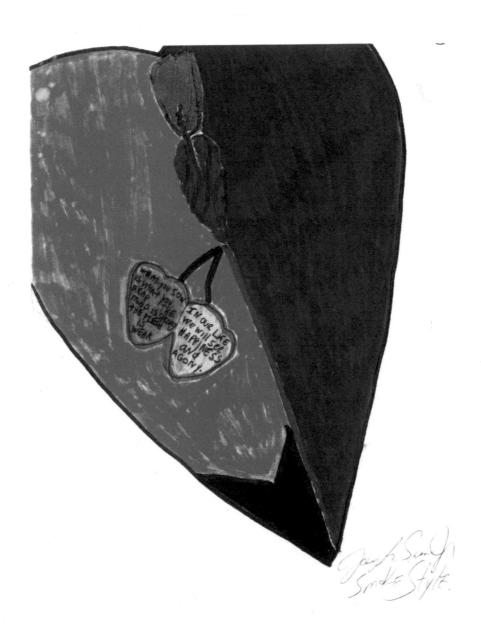

# What's up, Baby?

Why you stepping on me?
What's up, baby?
I know what's wrong
I've been quiet too long
But everything will change
You're the one insane
I got more juice than you could ever dream of having
You don't know what time it is—quit bragging
I'm harder than nails
Strong as a bull
Now you tell me
Can you touch these jewels?
More talents than you can imagine
I'm tired of you stepping on me
You have been the thorn in my side
Now I'm speaking up and it's all the way live
You hurt me, shut me up for years
I'm going to beat you down, yeah, you will fear
Why have you been stepping on me?
What's up, baby?
All my life I have been trying to find
Reasons why I had a blue mind
It's you, you are the culprit
I'm gonna tear your heart out
Get right in your face
What can you do to me?
I've already been disgraced
I want to knock you out and stump on your grave
For having me feel the pain of a slave
It's not a wrong thing; it's a right thing
Make a person change, too
I know why the caged bird sings
What makes you think you can say anything and not hurt another?

You look at me in my face and call me brother
So what I'm saying is the game is over
I won, you see, and I'm going to ask you again
What's up, baby?

# Reap What You Sow

What you sow
Is what you reap
The mind is strong
The flesh is weak
In our life
We will see
Happiness
And agony

# Mama

The most powerful lady on the earth
No one can pay her what she's worth
Without Mama's love, I never would have gone far
It's her love for her child
That she can pick up a car
Lift it right off her child
Will have no more joy in her life
Until she can see you smile
She will go up against the devil himself
Fight him to her very last breath
Come back from the state of death
If Mama's child needs some help
There's no one who holds a higher title
Or anyone who deserves our greatest love
Than the only person on earth
Whom we deeply call MAMA

Smoke

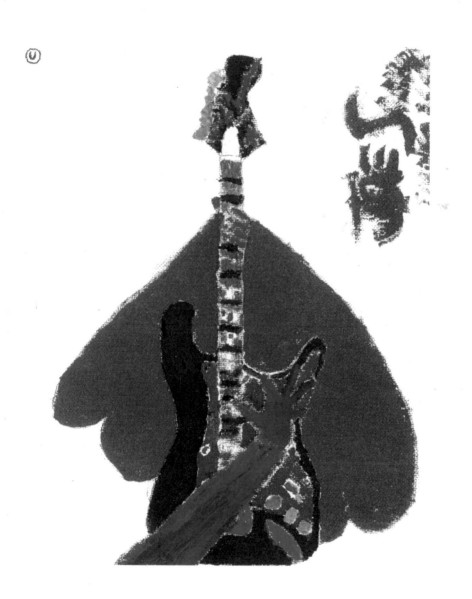

# Urban Man

Everybody has a story to tell
And mine sure ain't easy
Trying to find my way in life
And it sure ain't easy.

Mama and Pop doing the best they can
But still can't make ends meet
It's time for me to give a helping hand
But it sure ain't easy.

Oh, God, if you can hear my plea
Please, oh, please, help me
I don't want to give up
Although I'm losing my strength
Things got to get better
I'm hoping and praying
Things got to get better.

Oh, God, can you hear what I'm saying?
In this world I see the rich and the poor
The rich getting richer and the poor getting poorer
I want to be happy in my life
So I'm doing the best that I can
Will there just be trouble for this Urban Man?
I haven't found the key yet to unlock the door
I need help. Oh, God, I can't stand the pain no more.

# Driver's Seat

I'm so glad I've finally let God in my driver's seat
Being a proud man, it was hard to ask for directions
I got lost on these mean streets
Knocked off my feet
Then God rescued me and I jumped!
Into the passenger's seat!

# Stream of Consciousness

I want the old Joe back
With my ego intact
Got to get going forward
Too much stress in my life
Got to exercise, get a wife
Fight, fight, fight
Don't give up
I want the old Joe back
Have to work, work, work
Have fun, go berserk
Nothing to it but to do it
Fly, fly like an eagle
It's about to be my turn
Gather up everything I've learned
I want my piece of the rock
Do it now; don't watch the clock
Everybody got their strong points
Things they achieved
Got to break out of this joint
Got to believe
Got to think positive
That's a better way to live
Somebody help me
I need support
I'm calling out to anybody
Open my eyes so I can see
I'm the type-A personality
A million things going on inside of me
But where there's a will, there's a way
Walking down the street
Today will be a better day
Maybe you will meet me
Everything must change; nothing stays the same
I'm going to work, work, work myself sane.

# You Are Surely Missed

Dad, sly as a fox
Gentle as a sheep
For sure, YOU ARE SURELY MISSED!
Wise as you are humble
The world betrayed you—I'm sure of this
Lifted me up when I stumbled
For sure, YOU ARE SURELY MISSED!
Stayed in the jungle heat
Sweet was the meat we would eat
Through BLOOD, SWEAT, AND TEARS
You trapped underneath your feet
It is hard to believe you're gone
I will always copy your love
Through the rain, I pray to be as strong
Soothing my pain, whenever I'm thinking of
You've helped me to write my "things to do" List
Oh, Dad, for sure, YOU ARE SURELY MISSED

Smoke

# Do I Have Talent?

To draw a line, a work of art
Finding sin is in my heart
Musical tones from Heaven above
Holy is where I can love
To share the art of poetic word
To lose it all in one phase
Sing out loud and blue
Thank my lucky stars, he's watching you
Pray on my knees
Draw a picture of our enemy
I can hear and see him
Roaring in a microfilm
Telling me, "I'll give you what you want
You don't need that other junk."
Draw a picture of paradise
Hoping I don't roll the dice
On my future hopes and dreams
Hope I see the one that's unseen
Jehovah, the maestro of creativity
Hit me hard, please, wake me

# *Life*

Life, Life, Life, Life
Life, Life, Life, Life
Life, Life, Life, Life
I don't know why I went through so many changes,
I don't know how I got myself into danger,
I guess I didn't know myself; I was a stranger.
Ever since I got out of high school
Life hit me like a cannonball,
I was trying to do the best I could,
But I still fell so very hard
My nerves gave out on me,
And I was shaking all around
Everyone but me could see
I was having a breakdown.

In the Jungles of Africa
A King is Picked Wisely
Even some in America
Are picked By THE Almighty
But A King must Be Humble
And not Hauty
HE must HAVE Love Insurmountable
A King CAN Be Young or Old
But JEHOVAH picks thE

Bold!

Smoke
Style

# My Boys

Unconditional love
Believe in God
In Heaven above

My boys
Smart as whips
My boys
Can give me a few tips

Jehovah God, please
Keep them in your arms
Happy, safe, secure
My boys, keep your charms

Think positive
You have my unconditional love
Believe in God
In Heaven above

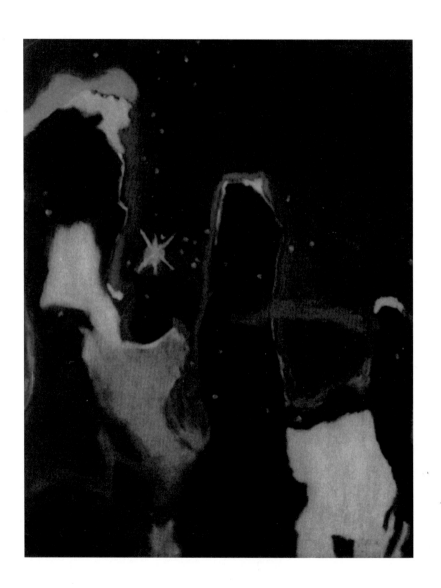

# Speak, Lord

I don't know where to begin
I am out on a limb
Swimming in my own vomit
Trying hard to admit

Find the Lord in my house
Afraid I might be the mouse
Speak, Lord, speak to me
Open my eyes so I can see

Find a woman in dirt
Must stay very alert
The trap is being set
Shall I not feel much regret?

My iron will is tough to crack
Lord, please watch my back
Speak, Lord, speak to me
Am I forever your enemy?

Marriage and then baby carriage
Sound very inviting to me
Ladies of night
Difference between wrong and right

Lustful eyes in want of heart
My own body is where it starts
Speak, Lord, speak to me
Thank you for opening my eyes to my misery

# This Year, 1990

One of the biggest things that has happened to me since the first of this year is I have started a relationship with my father. I didn't have one before because I isolated myself from my father, not expressing my feelings or dreams. Now I feel us growing closer, and I am beginning to understand his love for me. And if it's in his power, he will do what I ask of him. I am looking forward to more communication, not just with my father but with all who come into my life. I see a new Joe emerging from the ashes with faith in God and self. I can accomplish and lead the kind of life that is fruitful. So I can say the very biggest thing that has happened to me this year is coming to know, love, and understand myself, realizing I'm no freak out of a sideshow. I'm a normal-feeling person with hopes and dreams.

# I'm Truly Blessed

I'm truly blessed
As a Jehovah's Witness
I'm reaching my goal
To saving my soul
But only a beginning
To fighting sin
No longer wanting milk
But longing for solid food
Jehovah has truly built me
In love from crude
I'm truly blessed
As a Jehovah's Witness
Slowly coming to know
The narrow road to go
Serving Jehovah as a goal
Fighting to save my soul
Fall down now and then
Always learning till the end
Christ is head of our congregation
Our elders shepherd us with kindness and patience
Jehovah's Witnesses have love written on their faces
Let the will of Jehovah take place.

# Positive

New train of thought
Different way to walk
Imagination and reality
Greater possibilities.

Not thinking of the bad
Not always feeling sad
To raise my self-esteem
Positive is my theme.

Let the sun shine through
Dreams will come true
I am ready to live
'Cause I'm thinking positive.

# The Fight

I'm searching my mind, looking for an answer
Although I know it's gonna take some time.

The search for peace of mind sure isn't easy,
But I have hope of finding some kind of peace in
all this madness.

Oh, God, please help me. I need your strength.
The fight has just begun.
I'm getting hit pretty hard, and a flurry of punches
seem like they won't stop.

So help me to move, to hit first, and share the victory,
`Cause there is an EVIL one after me.